STEAM MEMORIES: 1950

No.7: SHEFFIELD to NOTTINGHAM the GC route

Including: Nottingham Victoria to Hucknall, Annesley,
Staveley & Darnall Sheds

BOOK LAW PUBLICATIONS

Copyright Book Law Publications 2008
ISBN 978-1901-945-645

Introduction.

The former Great Central Railway route from Sheffield (Victoria) to Weekday Cross junction in Nottingham, via Staveley, has been well chronicled in reputable railway histories, geographical surveys, and various photograph albums. This particular album captures, in the main, the last two operational decades of the GC line, some of its junctions and feeder routes and engine sheds. The photographs are mainly the work of the late Don Beecroft with, at the beginning, some of the late Keith Pirt's black & white production covering the middle fifties.

Locomotives in all their guises and conditions are illustrated at work, at rest and in retirement. Trains are featured on the line and in the stations. The run-down of this route is evident in some views whilst in other scenes it beggars belief that so much could have been got rid of so quickly through official vandalism.

This album is just one of a series which looks at British Railways during the last two decades of steam working. Besides the potted line histories and observations, there are also a number of albums dedicated to particular railway towns such as Crewe, Doncaster, Derby, to name but a few. There are many more either in the pipeline for future publication or already in production.

(above) **Don Beecroft in his younger days and (right) in his more mature years video recording the preserved steam at Butterley.**

(title page) **B1 No.61316 waits for the off at Nottingham (Victoria) with a southound express from Sheffield to Leicester in October 1958. Is that a wheeltapper by the BR Mk.1 Brake?**

Printed and bound by The Amadeus Press, Cleckheaton, West Yorkshire.
First published in the United Kingdom by Book Law Publications, 382 Carlton Hill, Nottingham NG4 1JA

Sheffield (Victoria) station, Sunday morning 26th June 1955. This is brand new BR Standard Cl.4 No.76058 on a running-in turn from Doncaster shed. The train is possibly a Liverpool-Hull working, the Cl.4 having just relieved an electric locomotive which brought the train from Guide Bridge. From here the 2-6-0 will take the train forwards to Doncaster where a Hull engine would take over the train. Not long out of Doncaster works, the Standard has already got a fair coating of grime on the new paintwork. Bound for the Southern Region, its initial allocation being Redhill, it was one of fifteen such locomotives constructed at the 'Plant' during 1955. This engine was to spend the whole of its short twelve year life on the Southern, Bournemouth, Eastleigh and Guildford also having its services until withdrawal in March 1967. The chimneys of Sheffield's Royal Victoria Station Hotel can be glimpsed just above the cab of the Class 4 whilst in platform No.1 a Nottingham 'local' awaits its next journey south. K.R.Pirt.

A fine view of 'Director' No.62660 BUTLER HENDERSON which, having just passed Sheffield No.5 signal box, is approaching Victoria station 'under the wires' whilst in charge of a stopping passenger train in 1954. This class of elegant 4-4-0 tender engines had by now been relegated to secondary duties such as this and, during the winter months especially, spent a lot of time in storage. No.62660 was based at Lincoln at this time, as were three other members of the class, one was at Immingham whilst the rest were in Manchester. By the early months of 1958 the whole class would have congregated at Darnall shed and all, except No.62663 which went to Staveley in April of that year, would finish their working lives at 41A. During the final couple of years up to their withdrawal the D11/1 class could be found working the stopping passenger trains between Sheffield, Nottingham, Chesterfield, Grimsby and Lincoln, just as depicted here. The end came for most of them in 1960, No.62665 had succumbed in 1959. BUTLER HENDERSON here achieved immortality and is, of course, part of the National Collection. K.R.Pirt.

One of Darnall's original O4's, No.63624, straddles the wet ash pit along with an unidentified Thompson B1 on 19th April 1954. Note that the 2-8-0 is wearing a 39B shedplate, Darnall's code prior to June 1955 when it became 41A and master of its own motive power area. The depot here was constructed and brought into operation during World War Two and its opening in 1943 was announced in the contemporary press under the strict censorship of the day as simply a 'New Locomotive Depot in the North Midlands'. Replacing the ancient edifice at Neepsend, Darnall was provided with all the modern amenities and appliances of the day, such as a coaling plant, 70ft diameter articulated turntable, wheel drop, lifting and machine shops, and this wet ash pit. This latter facility was a favourite of the LNER and its like had been installed at most of the important depots throughout the railway - Colwick, Eastfield, Gorton, New England, York, amongst others, and in BR days Thornaby. The wet ash pit was a simple solution to a large problem at any locomotive depot. The only drawback was the initial large capital investment which also included having a grab crane to empty the ash. The LMS had specialised in the overhead mechanical bunker which hoisted ash from the below rail pits into wagons, at first, but later models included a storage bunker much like a small coaling plant. Here the ash and clinker was simply thrown (shovelled) onto the moveable metal grids which allowed the debris to fall through into the water below. To enable ashpans to be raked out below rail platforms were positioned such that they enabled the 'pitmen' to rake ash directly into the cooling subterranean water. The O4, already forty years old when this picture was taken, was rebuilt to a Part 8 engine at Gorton in early 1955 and returned to Darnall in its new guise with a Diagram 100A boiler and side window cab but retaining its original cylinders. Condemned in December 1962, it was one of the few O4 class engines scrapped at Derby.

C13 class No.67439 had been a resident of Darnall shed for exactly a year when this pose was captured on 19th April 1954. Except for a three month stint at Bradford during late 1941, the 'Atlantic' tank had never been east of the Pennines working instead over the Cheshire Lines for much of its life until transferred to 39B on Sunday 19th April 1953. Darnall shed was to be its last home but its demise was some time off yet and the locomotive would undergo both a 'General' and a 'Casual Light' repair before being withdrawn and then cut up at Gorton in November 1958. Here the 4-4-2T was heading a line of locomotives on one of the ten stabling roads at the south end of the shed. Note that the coaling plant in the background was a compromise on the usual 'Cenotaph' like design mechanical coalers erected for the LNER in the 1930's, it was also of a much smaller capacity at 250 tons against 500. K.R.Pirt.

So far during this April 1954 photographic visit around the depot, Darnall shed has yielded only former Great Central locomotive designs for our camera but what would you expect from this place which managed, virtually to the end of steam at 41A, to keep hold of large numbers of the Robinson masterpieces. J11 No.64360 (just look at that pile of coal - slack - it has got to manage on next time out on the road) was another Darnall resident and was looking fairly clean for a locomotive associated to a depot not renowned for its cleanliness. The 0-6-0 had been transferred here from Retford shortly after the new depot opened for business and it was to stay until withdrawal. Surprisingly, that event was not long after this pose was caught, and in July 1955 it entered Gorton works for an expected 'General' and was instead condemned. But, at fifty-one years old that was not a bad innings. In medium sized freight locomotive terms, this engine had been around somewhat. From Langwith Junction shed it was transferred to Neasden in April 1927 but two months later it was reallocated to Cambridge where it settled for a couple of years prior to returning to 'Coal Country' at Annesley shed in October 1929. After seven years at Newstead it moved over to Colwick but was only there a week before Retford required its services in April 1936. In the right background of the picture the Craven's rolling stock factory holds the ground on the opposite side of the main line. K.R.Pirt.

The writer offers apologies to readers for presenting yet another ex GCR locomotive for your delectation. This is N4 No.69225 with the bunker of N5 No.69312 muscling into the picture on 19th April 1954. Both engines were Darnall residents, the N4 since 18th December 1949 when it arrived from Mexborough. The sixty-five year old 0-6-2T had been allocated to Darnall once before, from 30th September 1943 to 16th February 1944 when it moved on to Barnsley for a couple of years. The engine had last had a General overhaul during February/March 1952 and by now it was getting close to another visit to Gorton. The inevitable happened in December, New Years Eve to be exact. The following day it was en route to the scrapyard at Gorton along with 69228, 69230 and 69232. All were Darnall based and represented the last four examples of their class. K.R.Pirt.

Just to prove my point about the J11's being able to burn any old coal, I present this view of No.64443 with a pile of what can only be described as 'tat'. We are still at Darnall but the date has changed to 17th October 1954. It had been eight months since this engine had last been to works, its pristine coat of shiny black paint is now no longer visible through the layers of grime. Its next visit would be in September 1957 and by then it will look as filthy as the 'tat' in the tender. Except for two weeks in 1943, this J11 had been a resident of Sheffield since June 1916 and would remain so until condemned in April 1962. The tall building behind the tender is the depot water tower complete with a pitched roof to protect the 100,000 gallons stored there.

Now here is a nice change, same shed, same end (where all the sun was from midday onwards), same wheelbase as the last engine but different origin - completely. The Ardsley based J6, No.64262 was resting on Darnall shed prior to working back home. Recently out of Doncaster works after receiving a General overhaul, the 0-6-0 still has a glimmer of clean paint about but not, I doubt, for much longer. Note the shunting pole thread through the right hand lifting eye. On the same road is J94 'Austerity' 0-6-0T No.68070 which was en route to Gorton from Immingham shed for a Casual Light repair which would detain it at the Manchester works until 8th January 1955. Considering this was November in one of the most industrialised areas of the country the light seems to be just about right for the exposure. The date is Sunday 7th November 1954. K.R.Pirt.

Now this is how we all remember the WD 'Austerity' 2-8-0, filthy, cabside number obliterated by dirt but nevertheless looking the part of a busy 8F freight locomotive. No.90458 was one of the original two-hundred surplus WD 2-8-0s purchased by the LNER from the Ministry of Supply. At the time this photograph was taken, 4th October 1953, the Vulcan Foundry built engine was allocated to Hull Dairycoates shed where it was to spend most of its working life. It ended its days at Goole shed where it was amongst the last of North Eastern Region steam and was one of the last examples of the class. It was cut up at Draper's in Hull during December 1967. Behind the tender of the WD can be seen the bridge of the flyover which brought engines onto Darnall shed from the Up side line which negated conflicting movements with other trains on the main line.

To finish off our visit to Darnall shed we present this nice view of local Thompson B1 No.61152 outside the east end of the shed just after midday on Sunday 4th October 1953. This 4-6-0 is proof that Darnall depot did clean certain of their charges because the engines last repaint was carried out in March 1953 after a 'General' at Darlington. Another Vulcan Foundry product, works number 5510 of May 1947, the B1 was just three years younger than the WD which had VF No.5047 of May 1944. There all similarity ended. Not as fortunate as the 2-8-0, No.61152 was withdrawn from Immingham shed in April 1964 and was sold for scrap to a Lancashire scrap metal dealer. Prior to that though the B1 was to spent much of its life working from Sheffield sheds. Arriving at Darnall in June 1947 from Gorton (where it had been run-in), it was resident until the end of September 1957 when it transferred to Doncaster. Seven weeks later it was back at 41A for a couple of years before moving onto former Midland metals at Millhouses (41C) depot. Less than eighteen months later No.61152 was back at Darnall shed for another two years before finally letting go of the 4-6-0 for good when Immingham required its services. K.R.Pirt.

12

Moving south from Sheffield now we get as far as Beighton in September 1954. Working a southbound freight containing coiled wire, steel bars and slabs, is Doncaster based Gresley O2 No.63944, a not unusual engine to be working over the ex GCR main line south of Sheffield. The photographer is standing on the track bed of the erstwhile Holbrook Colliery branch, the truncated siding with a wagon on can be seen at the extreme left of the picture and were the only remains of the branch line at this time. The colliery itself was situated about a mile south of this spot and had access to both the GC and Midland Railway's 'Old Road'. Immediately behind the camera was the Meadow Gate Lane footbridge, a favourite venue for local enthusiasts (colloquially known as Cow Lane) and from where easy access to the nearby Midland line could be got. The MR line ran parallel to the GC at this point and was just east of the embankment on the right. Just a few hundred yards to the south the GC crossed over the Midland and carried on the same southerly course, with each vying for the coal traffic from the numerous collieries connected to the route. The GC line, like the colliery branch and indeed all the collieries in the area, is now just a memory. The O2 had been given a General overhaul and repaint during the previous May although to look at it the engine appears not to have seen a paint brush in years. However, the 2-8-0 had nearly seven more years of working life in front of it at this stage, including two more major overhauls, and a transfer to Retford in February 1957. Built at Doncaster in April 1924, it was to be dismantled there when condemned in April 1961.

13

Darnall based B1 No.61056 slows on the approach to Staveley (Central) station with a Sheffield (Victoria) - Nottingham (Victoria) stopping train in May 1960. note the good smattering of Gresley coaches making up the five-coach formation. The main line was blessed with four tracks through Staveley, the station itself originally had three platforms with four faces but in latter years the most easterly platform fell into disuse and access from the public road was cut when the Lowgates road bridge (A619) was rebuilt circa 1960. The B1 is running on what was then the Up fast line with the Down fast alongside. The two tracks east of the train were essentially the goods lines although freight trains used all four tracks, as did express passenger trains when necessary, however, speed restrictions were probably in force over the goods lines. Amazingly between the date of this photograph being taken and late 1962, all four main line tracks were re-laid from the bullhead rail seen here to flat bottomed rail. Once again it begs the question of costs, plans, accountants, and statistics! Filling the sidings on the right are loaded 16-ton mineral wagons with the produce of the area - coal. On the left is a rake of loaded iron-ore tipplers waiting to be taken into the Stanton iron works for discharge. Called Staveley Town up to 1950 and Central thereafter, the station opened 1st June 1892 and closed 4th March 1963.

At Staveley motive power depot in March 1959, two former GC engines and with the tender of another in view, stand outside the running shed. O4 Part 8 No.63884 had recently (January and February 1957) been rebuilt from a Part 7 engine and had benefited from a side window cab and a more modern Diagram 100A boiler being fitted. Complete with a shunters pole the 2-8-0 is resting on shed between turns of its usual job of working the colliery lines in the area. Alongside is J11 No.64384, also a resident of 41H, as Staveley GC shed was then coded. Unlike the O4, which was to leave Staveley for Mexborough shed in January 1960, the 0-6-0 worked from Staveley up to withdrawal in June 1961 ending an association with this depot which dated from March 1939. Prior to that No.64384 had been employed mainly at East Midlands sheds except for two interesting episodes when it left GC metals. The first was during World War One when in November 1917 it was sent to France in a bid to help the Allied war effort. Returning in June 1919, it was sent to Langwith Junction shed until September 1925 when it spent three weeks at Colwick. The second episode away from its usual sphere of operation saw it sent to the former Great Eastern shed at Cambridge but seventeen months later it returned north, this time to Colwick for a five month stint. In August 1929 Leicester shed had the 0-6-0 for one week then it went back to Colwick. Woodford shed became its home from February 1930 until February 1937 when Colwick got it back. The 2-8-0 also had a fairly interesting allocation history with GC and GN sheds having its services throughout most of its thirty-seven year working life. However, it was sent to work on the Great Western in November 1940 as part of the war effort of the next conflict. From the GWR, in January 1943, it then ventured up to Scotland, via a two week lodge at Woodford, transferring to Thornton Junction shed. It came back from Scotland nine months later and went to Doncaster shed. No.63884 ended its working days at Frodingham shed where, in June 1964, it was condemned and sold for scrap a few weeks later. A nearby scrapyard at Beighton carried out the cutting up.

By May 1960 Staveley engine shed had become a dumping ground for Sheffield Darnall's 'unwanted'. The classes involved included D11 'Directors', Gresley K3 and the same designer's K2 class, amongst others. Here tucked away at the rear of the depot, out of sight of the main line, was K2 No.61728 with No.61747 keeping it company. Alongside that K2 was another, No.61761, which had returned to Darnall from a 'General' at Cowlairs in September 1958 and had apparently never gone back into traffic except for a few weeks in the winter of 1960 prior to transfer to King's Cross. The transfer never took place and the engine entered Doncaster works to be condemned. No.61728 and 61747 were no luckier and went to Doncaster in December 1960 for scrapping. In this view the old rear wall of the original engine shed can be seen. Built by the Manchester, Sheffield & Lincolnshire Railway in 1892, the shed had twelve roads under cover of its northlight roof but in 1951 BR decided to take down what was left of the roof and reduce a newly covered section to the five most westerly roads. The tracks on which these stored engines are stabled were once inside the shed (note the paving between the filled-in pits). The scene is reminiscent of so many depots throughout BR at this time.

We are still at Staveley GC shed in May 1960 looking now in a north-westerly direction towards the main line. The new shed building with its lofty walls rears above the stored and stabled engines spread over the five outside roads on this east side. The tall coaling stage is still busy, no mechanical aids being provided for this depot. In front of the throng is 'Director' No.62661 GERARD POWYS DEWHURST, complete with its nameplates. K3 No.61973 is alongside the D11, whilst WD No.90070, along with another of the class and an O1, is stabled behind. The WD is a visitor from Frodingham and very much operational. Its demise did not occur until the end of February 1965. Note the once squared-off and carefully constructed coal stack is now being eaten into, the larger lumps being the prize whilst the slack is left behind. Staveley depot outlived all of the mentioned locomotives here (just). It closed for business in June 1965 and was afterwards demolished.

On the west side of Staveley engine shed an O4 Part 8 rests for the weekend. No.63899 was another of the former Ministry of Munitions 2-8-0s built by the North British Locomotive Co. in 1919 and purchased by the LNER. It entered traffic in June 1927 at Woodford shed and served that establishment until May 1944 when it came to Staveley for the first time. In October 1947 it moved to Annesley and then shuffled between there and Colwick until May 1950 when it went to Gorton shed. June 1953 saw it return to the East Midlands but at Colwick shed once again, however, at the end of November 1953 it went back to Staveley which was to be its final depot. Between June and September 1955 it was rebuilt to a Part 8 engine and was amongst the last of those rebuilds. The new guise enabled the engine to work for another eight years, with the help of a Heavy Intermediate overhaul in October 1961. The end for this 2-8-0 came in May 1963 and it entered Doncaster works at the end of that month never to come out. This side of the shed housed the offices, mess rooms and workshops and had managed to keep the original northlight roof covering. The roof of the lean-to against the wall of the shed contained equipment used by the fitters employed to keep the depot's fleet in service. Just behind the camera, to the right, was a set of shearlegs which enabled the depot to change locomotive wheels and get to bearings which would otherwise require a locomotive to visit main works for repair. Besides being self sufficient in the mechanical stakes, the shed also had its own gas works on the eastern side of the yard, alongside the Ireland Colliery branch. Over on the other side of that branch the MS&LR also had a large number of terraced houses (in excess of 100) for its personnel which were then on the leading edge of the London Extension. Six, more desirable, semis' with gardens front and rear were provided to the north of the station for the company officers running the show at Staveley.

Moving on from Staveley we stop, turn, and look north again back along the GC formation towards Tibshelf Town station in May 1965. The photographer has his back to the Midland line which ran from Mansfield Woodhouse to Westhouses on the Erewash Valley main line and which passed under the GC at this point. In the left distance can be seen the goods shed and signal box situated just south of Tibshelf Town station. Opened in January 1893, the station closed on 4th March 1963. The area was pure mining country, to the right of the train was the former Tibshelf Colliery, closed in 1939 before nationalisation of the coal industry in 1947 but still, some twenty-six years later, leaving a huge blot on the landscape, in the shape of the heap containing seventy years of spoil, seen above the front of the train. The train being hauled by WD No.90719 is a long rake of iron ore empties from the Stanton & Staveley works bound for the quarries near Melton Mowbray. The 2-8-0 is one of Staveley's own and although new to that depot, arriving in March 1965, it was to move on to Langwith Junction shed in June. This particular 'Austerity' was one of those purchased by British Railways who put it into traffic in September 1949 working from Wakefield shed. From there it transferred to Canklow in August 1959 before moving south to Staveley. Withdrawal took place in February 1966.

Just by Annesley engine shed (seen faintly through the gate on the left of the picture, and at a slightly lower level) there once existed two passenger railway stations, neither of which belonged to the GCR. The GC's own station which served this rural setting, Hollin Well & Annesley, was situated some distance to the north of the engine shed (opened in November 1901, closed 10th September 1962, there is some speculation that the place was not used by the public on a continuous basis and that it rarely featured in public timetables). Of the stations adjacent to the locomotive depot, the nearest was the former Great Northern Railway station which had opened in October 1882 and was called Newstead & Kirkby later changing to Newstead for Kirkby. It became Newstead & Annesley in 1889. The Midland Railway station, just slightly to the west and south was simply Newstead. Later additions to their names saw the GN station becoming Newstead East and the Midland establishment Newstead West. The MR station had in fact opened in 1863 but until 1883 was used privately but on 1st July that year it became a public station. The GNR station was used by the public until 14th September 1931 when the place was effectively closed and from that date only railwaymen working at the shed or nearby marshalling yard could use the station. Of course it was from this location that the famous 'Annesley Dido' used to run to and from Bulwell Common station and in this August 1946 photograph we present the push-pull train standing at the 'closed' Newstead East Up platform with F2 No.7105 (pre 1946 No.5777) in charge. Over the years of the 'Dido' workings, the motive power used has been extremely varied and always interesting. This particular engine was new to Annesley shed in August 1945 and had been previously fitted with push-pull gear in July 1937 for working the Dinting-Glossop branch. However, No.7105 was condemned in August 1948 leaving the door open for others of its kind to take over the duty. Sure enough, Annesley shed had a second F2, 7106, waiting in the wings but another F2, No.7107 was also available as stand-by engine. More F2 tanks came and went, No.7110 (ex5782) had been at Annesley since 1942 (the first F2 to arrive) but it was condemned in October 1947. By the summer of 1949 the short reign of the F2 class working the 'Dido' was over - just seven short years was all they managed prior to going for scrap. Time to bring on another class on its last legs. The 'Dido' story is long, complex, interesting and colourful but it is not in the remit of this album to present that history here so we have to leave Newstead but before we do it is worth relating that railwaymen stopped using the ex GNR station in March 1963. The GN signal box closed much later on 26th May 1968, colliery business taking it through another five years. The ex MR station closed in October 1964 but the Down platform has since reopened in a refurbished and modern guise as part of the Robin Hood line infrastructure. The GN station has gone along with the engine shed, and the adjacent Newstead Colliery - only the iron bridge of the Leen Valley line remains. However, if you frequent the platform of present Newstead station on a dark, cold and windy night it is possible to hear in the distance the shrill whistles of steam locomotives as they work through Nottinghamshire's Newstead estate along any one of the three parallel routes which must have made this place so very interesting all those years ago.

Annesley engine shed May 1960. Here is a line-up of motive power one would expect to see on visiting this depot - J39, O1, WD and B16. The latter two types were visitors, the WD 2-8-0s, the tender of one is just visible on the left, would turn up from Colwick, Staveley GC, Langwith Junction, Hull Dairycoates, to name but a few of the sheds sending them here to bring or take coal away from the nearby concentration sidings. Considering Annesley had none of the Austerity types allocated, the last examples came and went in 1951, there was always a large number about the yard. The B16, No.61419 on this particular day, was one of a couple which were daily visitors from York. Nearly always, York sent their original B16 (part 1) rather than the rebuilt examples. This engine had spent nearly all of its life working from York shed with just four short-ish excursions away - measured in months - at places such as Scarborough, Dairycoates, Neville Hill and Selby. When photographed at Annesley the 4-6-0 still had nearly sixteen months of operational life in front of it during which time it would get even dirtier than as seen here. It was condemned at the end of September 1961 and taken to Darlington works in mid October to be cut up. The resident Thompson O1 was a great favourite here and the number of them allocated during the early fifties' never really fell below fifty. However, their association with the depot was stretched twice up to their virtual cull in 1962. Firstly, in 1957, gradually, almost covertly during the year, twenty-five of them were exchanged for the BR Standard 9F 2-10-0 which on the face of it does not seem a bad swap at all - good for good. Another five disappeared to Colwick shed during that year, leaving just twenty-two. They all went in November 1962 after the London Midland Region take-over. Stanier 8F 2-8-0s came in and the Thompson O1 class engines were condemned, some had only returned from General overhauls just days before the LMR axe fell. It was certainly a huge waste of money to have withdrawn the 'foreign' engines so prematurely - criminal even. To add insult to injury the Thompson engines were sent to the LM works at Crewe and Derby for cutting up. The J39 at the end of the line is No.64798 which was withdrawn a month before the O1 debacle. This aspect of Annesley shed is the view north-westward from the middle of the yard. To the left can be seen the headframes of Newstead Colliery, next we have the water storage tank with the conical-roofed softening plant alongside. Finally the old coaling stage with a colliery spoil heap behind it. The coaling stage was superseded by a mechanical coaling plant during LNER days but the former stage was kept any emergency, a reflection of the one-time importance of this former Great Central depot.

Another York B16, No.61456, with a visiting WD for company, rests on Annesley shed yard for the weekend. This view is taken looking in a south-westerly direction with the six-road shed building behind the locomotives to the right. On the ground to the left of the 4-6-0 can be seen a base of one of the oil tanks erected during the ill-fated post-war fuel-oil fiasco. Immediately behind the B16 is a lone tender which was one of those fitted with a large steel snowplough. These independent snowploughs could be coupled to any vacuum ejector fitted locomotive and were stationed at strategic depots around the country. This particular vehicle has the legend 'Annesley' painted on the rear panel and appears to be of Great Northern origin. Visiting the site of Annesley engine shed today, one would be hard pressed to orient oneself as to what stood where. Most of the shed yard is now buried beneath a large mountain of colliery spoil.

Mention earlier of the Annesley Dido brings this locomotive, No.41280, into focus. The ex LMS Ivatt Cl.2 tank engine was one of a pair employed on the push-pull service during the latter years of its existence. This and the other Cl.2 No.41320, allocated to Annesley for the job (they arrived in January 1960 and December 1959 respectively) were superseded in March and April 1962 by three! of the BR Standard version of the same design, Nos.84006, 84007 and 84027. But their employment came to an abrupt end just a year later when in March 1963 the 'Dido' service was withdrawn after more than sixty-years of day-in, day-out running.

Before we leave Annesley and continue our photographic journey, we must look at a most unusual episode in the history of the depot when, between September 1962 and February 1964, no less than fifteen ex LMS 'Royal Scot' 7P 4-6-0 express passenger locomotives were allocated. In 1962 the London (Marylebone) to Sheffield and Manchester through expresses were withdrawn because other routes and services were available to those cities. However, en route between those places were other cities such as Leicester and Nottingham which only had the Midland main line services catering for them. Therefore it was decided to continue the curtailed services from Nottingham (Victoria) to Leicester (Central) and on to Marylebone using semi-fast timings. To run those trains the authorities allocated, from June 1962, four 'Britannia' Pacifics - 70014, 70015, 70048 and 70049 - to Annesley which up to that time had been involved mainly with the movement of freight. So, the scene was now set for accelerated and more frequent services to London from Nottingham via the GC main. Annesley had a new role to perform and some sort of engine cleaning occasionally took place although heavy maintenance was carried out at Midland shed in Nottingham. All went well until October when the four 'Brits' were whisked away to Willesden in exchange for a handful of clapped-out 'Royal Scots'. In anticipation of the conjuring trick with the Pacifics, the first of the 4-6-0s, Nos.46112 (appropriate), 46143 (from store), 46153 and 46158 arrived in September and then whoosh went the 'Brits'. Immediately more 'Scots' were drafted in, No.46126 in November and 46122 in December. In that same month No.46153 went down condemned. The 4-6-0s were really rough riders and at speed they began to border on being dangerous. Luckily timings were for semi-fast trains but still that entailed acceleration between the various stops. Further examples of 'Scots' then arrived in January 1963: 46101, 46111, 46163 and 46169. The condemnations continued with the last arrival being withdrawn four months later. During the summer things settled down a bit but in August No.46101 was withdrawn followed in September by 46111 and 46126. No.46114 arrived and was condemned immediately! Others coming to take their place in September 1963 included 46125 and 46167 followed by 46156 in October. In December No.46143 went and another, No.46165 took its place in February 1964. This was the last one, the junk cupboard was now empty but still the withdrawals continued with No.46167 in April, 46112 in May, 46163 in August, 46125 in September and finally 46122 and 46156 in October and 46165 in November. The picture shows No.46163 and 46125 in November 1964, awaiting a call for scrap. They look a sorry bunch indeed. Nos.46122 and 46165 had actually been reallocated in October and November respectively, before they were condemned, but those transfers did not take place - nobody wanted them. As far as the, by now lightly-laden semi-fast London trains were concerned the Annesley Stanier Class 5 4-6-0s took them over and worked them to the end of those services on the Great Central route. Of course, we must not forget the two 'Jubilee's' which also became part of the Annesley allocation at the same time as the 'Scots'. The first was a bog-standard 6P, No.45626 which arrived in November 1962 but left unexpectedly during the following January. Next came one of the two 7P rebuilds, No.45735 which came in October 1963 and put in nearly a full year of work before giving out in September 1964 when it was condemned.

Hucknall Central station was another of the GCR island platform affairs with all the essential buildings and amenities situated on one platform. In August 1964 the place was closed and deserted (*above*) when BR Standard Cl.9F No.92132 came storming through with a northbound special working. Closed on 4th March 1963, the place is still very much intact but the grass has started to take a grip in the cracks between pavement and tarmac although the flat roof of the canopy looks remarkably clean and clear compared with many flat roofed structures in the UK. The GC main line was the route virtually guaranteed to have at least one of these magnificent and powerful ten-coupled goods engines working a passenger train of sorts during summer weekends. (*opposite*) On the same Saturday afternoon the Poole-Sheffield (Victoria) was in the care of V2 No.60976 which is trying to obliterate the background with a good helping of smoke. Hucknall could at one time boast to having three railway stations, one for each of the companies which passed through before Grouping. First along came the Midland in October 1848 but they moved their first station to a new position south of the original in December 1895. It was called simply Hucknall. In 1952 the LM Region added Byron and the station closed as such in October 1964. Next through were the Great Northern who opened their station in October 1882. It too was called Hucknall but in 1923 the suffix Town was added. In the LNER's drive to cut costs in the depressed pre-war period and having duplicated facilities in the town, the station was closed to the public in September 1931 but continued to be used by railwaymen (for the Dido) until the late fifties. Finally, in March 1899 the Great Central opened their station which was known from the start as Hucknall Town. In 1923 it changed its name to Hucknall Central and remained so to closure. Since those depressing days of the Beeching era a kind of sanity has returned to transport planning and on 17th May 1993 the former Midland station was re-opened as part of the Robin Hood line initiative and since then the place has thrived having, the Nottingham Express Tram station built alongside.

Bulwell Common sidings was not a place where one could often, if ever, see a 0-4-0 + 0-4-0 narrow gauge articulated - Improved Meyer? - side tank. However, in August 1953 this new W.G.Bagnall Ltd. product was securely positioned on a BR wagon whilst en route to either Hull or Immingham for export. It is believed the customer was the owner of sugar plantations in Natal, South Africa and that two such locomotives had been built by Bagnall's. The specified gauge was 2ft 0½in. and the works numbers were 3014 and 3015 but it is unknown which particular one this was. Apparently plates bearing the names MBOZOMA and SINKWAZI were fitted after delivery as were headlights in front of the chimney. As can be seen, a round marine type firebox or 'Bull Head' boiler was employed for this locomotive because of the limited clearance between the rear power bogie and the firebox. This type of firebox apparently required a different style of firing method compared to that employed when shovelling coal into a more orthodox deep firebox. A similar locomotive was also built by Bagnall's in 1953 for the Bowater's Paper Mills Ltd company in Kent but it was made to 2ft 6in. gauge. It would be interesting to know the route taken from Stafford to Bulwell with this 28 ton load but my guess is via the GNR from Stafford Common, through Derby to Basford North.

The WD 'Austerity' 2-8-0s served this route from their wartime introduction and 'loan' to the LNER in 1943, through the post-war LNER period and throughout the BR era. Their comings and goings were daily and often, especially towards the end of steam when older classes were being withdrawn and the fairly young 'Austerity' just kept going. No.90001 is just south of Bulwell Common with a Down train of empty mineral wagons bound for either Newstead Colliery or another of the Leen Valley pits. The engine was on loan to Colwick shed for a month during October and November 1965 from Doncaster shed, note the AWS for East Coast main line workings. No stranger to the area, No.90001 was allocated to Annesley for five months during 1951 and in December of that same year it moved to Colwick from Staveley for a six year stint. Its end came six months after this action was captured on film.

On a pleasant late April evening in 1960 a Dairycoates K3, No.61927, runs a fish train from Hull Up the GC main towards Nottingham. Basically coasting downhill from hereon, the 2-6-0 has just passed over the GN line and is fast approaching Bagthorpe junction. Where the train was bound is unknown but it was certainly a long one, and smelly for those who remember their passing. Nowadays any fish landed at British ports, and it is not a lot compared with the sixties for instance, is taken away by road or goes into local processing plants. Which ever way you look at it, the fish train is yet another memory long gone and probably lost to the rails forever. This K3 had been allocated to Dairycoates since January last and it was to be its final posting before entering Doncaster works in July 1961 for cutting up.

In July 1960 the D11 'Directors' were just about keeping going and No.62662, in appalling external condition, is seen leaving Bulwell with a Sheffield (Victoria) - Nottingham (Victoria) 'local'. Note that the coaching stock of this train is all ex LMS yet it was on the same diagramming as the Sheffield-Nottingham 'local' shown being hauled by B1 No.61056 at Staveley (Central). In this make-up are four corridor coaches with two suburban vehicles behind. The same train on the next evening brought No.62662 again but this time with a combination of three Gresley coaches, a BR Mk.1 Open and two suburban vehicles. The PRINCE OF WALES nameplate is still attached to the 4-4-0 along with half a ton of grime but the life of this engine was rapidly drawing to a close. On 8th August it was condemned and consigned to Doncaster for cutting up.

Coming up the grade out of Nottingham and crossing over the GN line at Bagthorpe junction in April 1960, was BR Standard 9F No.92032 with a train of flat wagons. Judging by its external condition, one would immediately comment that this was an Annesley engine, although to be fair most sheds neglected their charges cleaning during this period. But you would be right about the 2-10-0s home shed, it was Annesley. By 1960 the fleet of ten-coupled engines had grown considerably at Annesley (amazing to recall that 92220 herself had only just been put into traffic). They were mainly employed on the Woodford 'runners' or 'windcutters' and were very good at that job too although, in reality, the job could have been done by two-thirds of the allocation. In 1965 this engine moved on to nearby Kirkby-in-Ashfield for a few weeks before joining forces with the surviving members of the class at Birkenhead. In the right background of this picture can be seen coaching stock stabled in Basford North carriage sidings, an installation created within the triangular layout of Bagthorpe junction. Before proceeding any further along the GC main we will now have a look around this interesting and somewhat dramatic location where the GC met the GN all those years ago and what became of that eventful meeting.

Swinging round Bagthorpe curve in the transition from the GC Down main to the GNR Derbyshire Lines at Basford East Junction, Ivatt LMS Cl.4 2-6-0 No.43159 heads down hill with a Nottingham (Victoria) to Derby (Friargate) 'stopper' in October 1958. Just here the gradient changes from a imperceptible 1 in 2590 to a steep 1 in 88 before the junction. On the left (high level) and right (lower level) are the Basford North carriage sidings laid in by the GNR when this junction complex was created in 1898.

Having travelled east along the former Great Northern Railway's Derbyshire & Staffordshire line, O4/7 class No.63770 runs tender first, through Basford (North) station and starts to negotiate Basford West junction with a mineral train bound for Colwick yard in February 1960. The signals are arrayed to give access to (viewed from the front, left to right) [1] the GC Down main via Bulwell south curve; [2] the GC Up main via Basford tunnel, the infamous 'Rathole' and Bagthorpe junction; [3] the 'main line' past Leen Valley junction, through Daybrook and Mapperley tunnel to Colwick (the so-called 'Back Line'). This latter route was to be closed just a few months later when a collapse inside Mapperley tunnel, during repairs, on 4th April made the bore unsafe and the direct route to Colwick had to be abandoned. Purchased from the Ministry of Munitions, the LNER put this engine into traffic in March 1928 at Hull Dairycoates shed and it was to spend all its LNER life working from depots in the North Eastern area. During the war, in June 1940, it was rebuilt to Part 7 standard acquiring a Diagram 15D. In September 1951 it was sent to Southall shed on the Western Region to help out during a motive power shortage but it only spent two weeks there before returning north. However, this time it went to the Eastern Region at Immingham for a seven year spell. No.63770 transferred to Colwick shed in December 1958 and a seven year stint working from there was also 'on the cards'. Withdrawn in December 1965, it was the last of the original forty-three O4 class Part 7. No.63770 was sold for scrap in February 1966.

L1 No.67758 enters Basford (North) with a midday Nottingham (Victoria) to Derby (Friargate) local in February 1960. The train has just passed under Park Lane bridge after traversing the south to west junction from the GC line at Bagthorpe junction. To the left of the engine is the spur to the GC main at Bulwell which was regularly used for turning locomotives. The Great Northern station here had an interesting history of different names throughout its existence. Opened as New Basford in February 1876, it was later renamed Basford & Bulwell. British Railways eventually renamed the place Basford North in 1953. It closed 7th September 1964. The signals on the right control the bay platform, which was often used by local trains up to closure. The left hand peg put trains onto the Bagthorpe junction line for Victoria station whilst the right hand peg put trains onto the 'back line' through Daybrook, Gedling and Colwick.

Having just accelerated down the 1 in 99 falling gradient from Basford North, Thompson B1 No.61381 now traverses a short level stretch of line as it approaches Basford tunnel, the 'Rathole', in July 1960. After 'turning' on the triangle of lines from Bullwell South junction, Basford West junction and Bagthorpe junction, the engine is now facing the right way for working home. From here the Leicester based 4-6-0 will make its way to Victoria station or perhaps New Basford carriage sidings to await its duty. This burrowing junction was created in 1898 to enable GNR trains to gain access to Victoria station without having to cross the GCR main line at Bagthorpe junction. The number of local passenger trains run by the GN from Nottingham and beyond to places such as Derby, Heanor, Pinxton, Ilkeston was high and their continuous southbound passage crossing the GC Down main would have created delays to the important GCR express passenger services, hence the expense. Above the cutting is the GN main line to Colwick although by this date it was no longer a through route and every train, passenger or goods, off the Derbyshire extension lines had to traverse this cutting and tunnel. Beyond the 'main line' is the carriage yard put in when the GCR came through Nottingham. In amongst the various carriage sidings was a turntable and ash pit where locomotives could be serviced for return passage without going onto Colwick shed. The B1 spent nearly all of its short eleven year life working from sheds situated on the old GC lines - Woodford, Leicester and Gorton - the two months residency of Colwick when new does not count.

A little later that day A5 No.69814, running bunker first, follows the same path as the B1 and starts to climb now as it dives beneath the skew bridge at the entrance to the narrow and confining 90 yard long 'Rathole'. From here up to Bagthorpe junction it is a 1 in 100 climb which the Pacific tank will take with ease. The A5 was one of the original Great Central, Gorton built engines which entered traffic between Christmas and New Years Eve in 1912. Starting life at Annesley shed, the 4-6-2 certainly knew its way around the Southern area of the LNER and the Eastern Region of BR, residing at eight different sheds between London and Bradford during its forty-eight year lifespan. When captured by Don Beecroft's camera in July 1960 it was newly arrived (2nd stay) at Colwick shed having come from King's Cross via Lincoln just a few weeks previously. This dramatic picture also captures something of the man-made geography of this place. At the top left of the picture is the GC main line bridging over the GN route, the gradient of the former being quite distinguishable from this vantage point. On the GN line is an empty iron ore train which has used its former route as a refuge whilst awaiting passage through the 'Rathole' and Victoria station to Weekday Cross en route to Colwick. The initial months of the Mapperley tunnel closure caused a lot of headaches and operations such as this were commonplace. No doubt about it though - the Great Central route and its Basford connections had saved the day. Beyond the line of wagons we have another aspect of the GN Basford North carriage sidings. Note the GNR concrete post somersault signal.

Continuing our photographic survey southward (slowly now because it gets much busier) we cross the main line and climb the rock cutting which separated Bagthorpe junction from the bridge carrying Perry Road. In June 1961 a Thompson L1, No.67753, hauls a Derby local on the last stretch of its journey down to Victoria station. Only New Basford to call at now before descending into another rock cutting and traversing two tunnels through the sandstone plateau on which much of the city of Nottingham was built. Compared with the Midland Railway and the GNR who were here long before them, the GC had a real battle to reach into the centre of Nottingham and, once there, an equally difficult task to get out of the other side and across the Trent. No.67753 had spent much of its life working out of the station which was the eventual goal of the GCR - London Marylebone. Shedded at Neasden, with five months at King's Cross thrown in either side of New Year 1950, the 2-6-4T transferred to Colwick in November 1958 and took up duties such as this quite successfully but diesel multiple units were waiting in the wings and so the Colwick L1 fleet was all but condemned in 1962, another decent design which came too late. This engine went in February 1962 during a visit to Darlington works for its bi-annual overhaul when instead it was condemned and then cut up.

Seen from the same vantage point a month later, is B16/3 No.61463 with a long train of new London Transport Underground stock for the District Line. The York based 4-6-0 will probably work the train as far as Woodford, perhaps even to Neasden LTE depot. Note that re-ballasting and sleeper renewal of the Up line has taken place during our short absence.

Going back in time now - not that far back - to August 1960. This picture could have been captured forty years previously but then the stock would have been different and the engine would have been extremely clean, shining even and it would probably be going a little faster too. This D11/1 'Director' No.62660 BUTLER HENDERSON is running over the main line which was its birthright. The elegance of the Robinson design is still there albeit looking somewhat shabby under a thick coating of grime but nevertheless the engine somehow appears to be totally 'at home' on this railway. However, the 4-4-0 would not last much longer, already six of its class had gone for scrap and the others would not be far behind them. As for this engine, well, the rest is history but it has certainly outlived its own native railway.

The shape of things to come on the Nottingham-Marylebone semi-fasts - the good old Stanier Class 5. But that was to be a couple of years in the future. It is now July 1961 and this is a returning Llandudno-Leicester (Central) holiday train negotiating the rock cutting to the north of Perry Road bridge. Look inside the tender of Leicester GC based No.44830 - virtually empty. The route taken by this train would have been quite interesting especially after Crewe where the North Stafford route to Kidsgrove would bring it into Stoke and from where the line to Uttoxeter was chosen to make Eggington junction and Derby Friargate. From there we know the way to Nottingham Vic, via the 'Rathole'. Since coming into traffic in August 1944 this Class 5 had certainly been around with residencies at Kentish Town, Bath, Newton Heath, and Millhouses already under its belt prior to transferring to Leicester GC in June 1960. From there it went to Derby in November 1963 then Colwick and finally Heaton Mersey from where it was withdrawn in August 1967.

Passing New Basford carriage shed on the climb up to Bagthorpe junction on Saturday 15th August 1964, this Western Region Collett 'Grange', No.6858 WOOLSTON GRANGE had charge of this Bournemouth-Bradford and Leeds train which was ex Nottingham (Victoria) at 2.40 p.m. It was unusual to see WR engines working trains north of Nottingham (they would sometimes run light engine to Annesley or Basford to turn) because of clearance problems, especially north of Sheffield (Victoria) so this working must have been necessary because of failure of the relieving engine. WR engines worked into Victoria every day after July 1964 because Leicester shed, which supplied the relieving engine at Leicester (Central) had by then closed and so the copper-capped 4-6-0s were allowed to work to Nottingham to change. Bringing trains from Oxford which had originated at various towns on the south coast they were taken off at Victoria in exchange for an Eastern Region engine. On this particular day failure had been the reason for No.6858 to remain on the front so off it set for pastures anew, albeit with an Annesley crew. At Sheffield it managed to damage the platform so the Bradford driver who was supposed to take over from there refused to have anything to do with engine after it was realised that no other engine was available to work onwards to Huddersfield. A Locomotive Inspector then took charge and off they went up to Penistone where the line to Huddersfield, through Denby Dale was taken. At the latter station the wooden platform was then assaulted by the cylinders of the 'Grange' so that by Huddersfield everyone had had enough. Luckily Hillhouse shed had a spare engine and the train went off to Bradford none the worse but running a little late. The 'Grange' was taken to Hillhouse shed where it spent a few days in remand whilst discussions took place as to what was to be done with it. It returned to the WR and to Nottingham a few more times after that but no more of its kind were allowed north of Annesley thereafter.

A month earlier this Skegness-Derby holiday train was captured climbing out of New Basford with Cl.4 No.43091 piloting B1 No.61210. With only eight vehicles behind the tender the load seems to be well within the capability of the 4-6-0 but line occupation was a big problem on this stretch of railway at the time so the extra engine was probably attached to get it over to Derby without too much fuss.

'Jubilee' No.45562 ALBERTA, complete with nameplate, slowly makes its way down the bank at New Basford in July 1964 en route to Victoria station to await a northbound train. The 4-6-0 has been up to Annesley depot for servicing and is now ready to work back home to Leeds. At the time this engine was allocated to Farnley Junction shed but moved back to Holbeck from whence it came earlier in the year. No.45562 was one of the longest-lived members of its class and was not withdrawn until November 1967. The backdrop to the picture is formed by New Basford carriage shed which had been another of the necessary investments by the GCR as they were pushing forward to their London goal.

Now here is a light load for a big engine. Peppercorn A1 No.60125 SCOTTISH UNION runs easily up the grade from New Basford with a Down parcels train in June 1964. Allocated to Doncaster shed since January 1958, the Pacific was just days away from being condemned and sold for scrap.

On Saturdays during August 1960 virtually everything (anything?) that could raise a good head of steam was pressed into passenger service on the GC main line. Annesley shed luckily had its large fleet of Standard 9F 2-10-0s to fall back on and these, once it was realised that they could also get up to a good speed, besides being able to haul anything, were used on many of the holiday trains traversing the route. No.92073 has charge of a seven vehicle Ramsgate to Bradford train which comprised a nice mixture of stock, and is seen passing New Basford on the climb to Bagthorpe.

Look at the length of that train, empty wagons admitted but nevertheless an impressive piece of tonnage and taken so easily up the grade by 9F No.92073. This was one of the returning 'runners' from Woodford to Annesley yard in July 1961. Impressive trains with impressive timings which, it was officially stated at the time, could have been bettered to make these engines even more efficient than they were. When Annesley shed finally gave up these ten-coupled Standards in 1965, most went north whilst this particular engine went south to the former Great Western shed Banbury, along with 92013, 92030, 92033, 92067, and 92074.

Having worked down (Up) from Sheffield (Victoria) with a stopping train, Darnall K3 No.61967 pauses at New Basford station in July 1960 before continuing downhill on the last leg of its journey into Nottingham Vic. The island platform arrangement at New Basford was typical of the London Extension stations built by the GCR. Opened on Wednesday 15th March 1899, it closed sixty-five years later on Monday 7th September 1964 without ceremony. The K3, an Armstrong Whitworth product of July 1936, met its end some time before in April 1961 when it was cut up at Doncaster works.

Later that day another K3, No.61813, comes charging up the bank from Sherwood Rise tunnel with a Nottingham (Victoria) - Ollerton stopping train. The 2-6-0 was at this time allocated to Hull Dairycoates shed although its state of cleanliness is hardly a clue as most engine sheds had given up the chore of cleaning their charges by this date. However, it is not known if the K3 was performing a filling-in turn from Colwick prior to working back to Humberside with a through train or it was making its way back home via this duty and then light engine to pick up a coal train from Mansfield concentration sidings. Note the flat bottomed rail used on this route, even the refuge sidings have been so laid. In the background an unidentified J39 shunts the New Basford goods yard when such things were an everyday occurrence. Line capacity between Bagthorpe junction and Weekday Cross junction was somewhat at a premium with the closure of the 'back line' and an extra seventy-six goods trains a day, to and from Colwick yard, used the route during the summer months of 1960. Add in the holiday extras and special excursions - an enthusiasts dream but a signalmans nightmare. So, what happened to all that traffic in so short a time? How was a very busy route suddenly made redundant?

47

Moving just a few yards south from our previous vantage point alongside the line at New Basford goods, we are next treated to the sight of a 'Britannia' getting into its stride up the 1 in 130 gradient out of the 665 yard long Sherwood Rise tunnel. The Pacific is No.70013 OLIVER CROMWELL from Norwich Thorpe, the train is a Bournemouth-Newcastle express. The date is 23rd July 1960, a Saturday. How the two became one is unknown to the writer and how the GE line engine came to be working on the GC main line is also a mystery. But, that was one of the enjoyable aspects of trainspotting - observing the unusual. Exciting stuff in those heady days when out-of-Region engines would suddenly appear. It was to be another three years and five months before No.70013 changed allegiance from the Eastern to Midland Region. The same length of time was to elapse before Immingham started to send its new allocation of 'Brits' on the New Clee-Banbury fish trains down the GC main line so this was quite rare. Apparently, No.70013 had worked the 8-35 a.m. Newcastle-Bournemouth (with SR stock) from at least York so this may well have been its return working (with normal coloured stock). How far the Pacific took the southbound train is unknown but Leicester is more than likely the turning point.

Our final view in the rock cutting outside Sherwood Rise tunnel shows B1 No.61000 SPRINGBOK hauling a Bournemouth-Sheffield holiday extra on 23rd July 1960. No.61000 was at that time allocated to Colwick shed and had probably taken over the working from a Western Region 'Hall' or 'Grange' at Nottingham (Victoria). Recently fitted with AWS at Stratford works, the 4-6-0 had spent much of its life working on the former Great Eastern lines between Cambridge, London and Norwich. It had transferred to Colwick from Doncaster on 12th June 1960 having arrived at the latter shed from March depot during the previous December. This engine was the class leader or prototype (although such things rarely if ever occurred in steam locomotive engineering) of a successful design which saw 410 B1 locomotives built from 1942 to 1952. Indeed when No.8301, as it was then numbered, was put into traffic in December 1942 it was to be six months before the next engine entered service so it could well have been regarded as a prototype. However, the delay in construction of further members of the class was not down to any trials or tests but instead it was the lack of materials, space and time - war work having precedence over everything, especially where materials and labour was concerned. This was Edward Thompson's best design even though it had V2 wheels, K2 cylinders, O2 chimney and a boiler which Gresley had endorsed in 1939. No.8301 was joined by four more of the class during 1943 but it was to be 1946 before full production started with the help of outside contractors. As No.61000 it was one of the early candidates for withdrawal and was condemned in March 1962. The third member of the class No.61002 (8303) IMPALA lasted five years longer and was sold for scrap in August 1967.

Even before it became famous for working special trains whilst in preservation, Gresley A3 No.60103 FLYING SCOTSMAN was often called upon to work railtours or parts thereof when in BR service. In April 1960 it had charge of a northbound Ian Allan Special on the GC line and called at Nottingham (Victoria) for water. Nicely cleaned for the occasion (34A always turned out its top link engines this way), the Pacific was no stranger to this main line and had often worked Manchester- London expresses through Nottingham both as an A1, in the dark days of 1944, when shedded at Gorton, and again during the early fifties when allocated to Leicester Central shed as an A3. Just prior to this particular outing the King's Cross based engine had gone through a Casual Light repair at Doncaster works. Note that the German trough type smoke deflectors have yet to be fitted.

The sun was never very favourable for photography at the north end of Victoria, the direct sunlight of the morning being masked by the huge train shed. Midday or early afternoon was probably the best period for capturing northbound departures in the platforms. It was just after midday in May 1960 when Darnall based B1 No.61056 was recorded at the head of the five coaches and four vans which made up the Nottingham-Sheffield (Victoria) stopping train. The station appears eerily quiet for such a vast place; something that had dogged Victoria for most of its existence and was, in the end, prove to be its undoing. The B1 was no stranger to Nottingham having spent five years at Colwick shed from June 1952 to October 1957 when it transferred back to Ipswich.

Leicester Central based BR Standard Class 5 No.73045 (*above*) is stabled on the turntable road at the south end of Victoria station, the Lower Parliament Street dock, awaiting a working which will take it back home in May 1960. The 4-6-0 was a regular visitor to Nottingham between September 1959 and June 1964, a period when it was allocated to various GC line depots; Neasden and Woodford Halse were the other establishments. After its time on the GC it transferred to Shrewsbury but undertook two more changes of shed prior to ending its days at Patricroft from July 1965 to August 1967. In August 1963, and looking somewhat cleaner (*opposite*) it was allocated to Woodford depot and was apparently in charge of the 8-15 a.m. London express but note that the departing platform (No.7) for this train is different from the usual No.10. Also, by this time, the normal stock for this train consisted fairly new BR Mk.1 vehicles whereas the Brake behind the tender is of LMS origin. Southerly departures from Victoria had a rather easier time than those going northbound because there was a falling gradient of 1 in 100 from the platform end to about midway through Victoria Street tunnel when the gradient changed uphill to 1 in 264 prior to 1 in 193 before Weekday Cross.

Still at the south end we look at the Grantham stopping train in platform No.11 on a June evening in 1960. At its head, K2 No.61756 is looking reasonable for a Colwick engine, although the Gresley 2-6-0 had not long been resident at the depot having arrived from Immingham shed on Monday 13th June. The painted embellishments were not a usual Colwick trademark so the engine must have been so adorned at Immingham prior to transfer. The load is hardly taxing for the K2, considering what it was capable and expected of hauling when new in 1918 but, this is the kind of work they were relegated to by the sixties. Since coming into traffic during the last summer of the Great War, No.61756 had been allocated to nine different sheds some, like Boston and Colwick, on three separate occasions, Doncaster and King's Cross twice. The latter depot will receive the 'Mogul' once more in January 1961 and it will work from there for another eighteen months before being condemned and sent into Doncaster works for cutting up at the ripe old age of forty-four. Although never allocated to a Scottish shed, Bradford being its most northerly posting, No.61756 was, since February 1944, regularly overhauled by Cowlairs works along with the rest of the class. The crew are nowhere to be seen (*opposite*) and the engine is left to simmer before departure time, obviously everything was okay with the locomotive with adequate supplies of coal and water. Note the former LMS coaching stock making up the train.

(*above* & *opposite*) Moving forward now to August 1962, we have two views of 'Britannia' Pacific No.70015 APOLLO standing on the turntable road waiting for its train, the 12-25 p.m. Marylebone, whilst the fireman tends to the indifferent coal in the tender. Luckily that big wide firebox was made to burn coal such as that so the day should not be too grim, just warm. APOLLO was one of four 'Brits' transferred to Annesley for the summer of 62, the others being Nos.70014 IRON DUKE, 70048 THE TERRITORIAL ARMY 1908-58, and 70049 SOLWAY FIRTH. All four of them had come from Neasden shed in June but when they left Annesley in October they returned to London but to Willesden depot instead. The age of the 'Annesley Scots' was dawning and the only other 'Brits' to use Nottingham Victoria after these four left in October was the Banbury fleet in 1965/66.

Seen from the loading dock ramp, the station pilot on that day was K3 No.61831, a Colwick engine which also had a tender full of dodgy coal but at least it would not be called upon to find reserves of energy for fast main line running with a heavy train. The K3 had but weeks of service left before withdrawal on 16th September. As can be seen the sun shone over this area of the station all morning so this end was the more popular one for enthusiasts. Cl.5 No.44984 hovers around platform No.1 whilst out of sight to the right and about to vacate platform 10 for the London train stock, was L1 No.67749 with the 11-30 a.m. local to Grantham.

We return to February 1962 and the 'Back line' is but a memory. All the goods trains wanting to gain access to Colwick yard and beyond from the west and north now have to travel through Victoria and Weekday Cross. The station has not seen some much traffic in decades but most of that is through freight traffic and only the signalmen are aware of any change. Having returned empties to one of the local pits, Colwick O4/3 No.63859 makes its way home with a brake van and is traversing No.7 platform road during a lull in passenger workings. This locomotive was another of the former Ministry of Munitions engines purchased by the LNER and put into traffic in 1927 as No.6620. From February 1929 it spent twenty-one years at Annesley shed but was sent to Gorton in exchange for a Thompson O1 in November 1950. It came to Colwick in June 1954 and worked from there until withdrawn in October 1963. The massive slab of sandstone surrounding this station is witness to the amount of civil engineering required to create this station and its infrastructure. For the period it was very well equipped operationally with a turntable and locomotive servicing siding at each end of the site. There was also four bay platforms at each end and four through platforms. Horse docks, with ramped access from the roadway, were also provided at each end so as to keep conflicting shunting movements down to a minimum. To complement the north and south signal boxes, each of the main island platforms had a signal box situated about midway along their length. If only the traffic had lived up to expectations, perhaps even grown beyond them. Would the tunnels have been doubled in number to cope with the traffic? Would the GC main line have been quadrupled? Would we now have a direct service to the Continent from the North of England and the East Midlands? The latter might have become a possibility if the GC main line had not been closed in the sixties but it was closed and so we have to live with the lost opportunities and dreams of what might have been. Luckily we still have the memories and the photographic record.

The winter of 1962-63 was one of the worst of the century, the snowfall in some areas was moderate compared with 1947 but the temperatures fell dramatically in November and remained at or below freezing for weeks at a time. By mid December British Railways was starting to feel the chill and much of its new diesel stock was failing due to frozen radiators. steam locomotive withdrawals slowed down and some condemned engines were brought back into traffic to make up for the stranded and useless diesels. Of course steam traction had to battle the elements too, water supplies had to be secured from freezing up, coal which had frozen in wagons had to be picked out and frozen points freed up. That winter was a very step learning curve for BR and the country as a whole. At Annesley shed their newly acquired batch of 'Royal Scots' might have been worn out and ready for scrapping - some thought - but at least they still worked and could be relied on to get the job done. (*above*) In January 1963, No.46101 albeit minus nameplates, stands in the freezing cold at the south end of No.7 platform having just come down from the shed. (*opposite*) This picture of Victoria in January 1963 has the winter scene summed up. There are four steam locomotives in view, three of them B1 class, and a solitary Stanier Cl.5 on the turntable road. All sorts of snow and ice clearing methods were used, the most popular being the steam lance fed from the carrying locomotive. It was during this big freeze that the manufacturers of point heaters suddenly got extremely busy but their appliances were no good for this season. It would be many years before all the relevant points, switches and turn-outs - call them what you like - were finally equipped to cope with such weather.

Our final snowy winter scene at Victoria in January 1963 shows another aspect taken for granted by most - keeping the water flowing. This is the water column at the south end of platform No.7 with its attendant brazier surrounded by ash and, note the new use for the platform baggage trolley as a coal carrier. Besides stopping the water from freezing, the brazier was a welcome sight for the hardy trainspotter who ventured out and, believe me, a lot of them did venture out during that long winter. 'Platform ending' was risky but the duffel coat and balaclava did help to stave off the polar-like cold. Pencils came into their own once again when the new fang'led biro froze. Technology lost out once again to the simple things in life. Oh yes, remember gazing into the cab of a waiting steam locomotive and wishing, hoping even, that the driver would invite you onto the footplate for a quick warm. Good old days? Well, yes because we had all those steam locomotives to 'cop' and new routes to travel over. Alongside the column is Stanier Cl.5 No.45270 and 44691 at the head of the 12-25 p.m. Marylebone express with steam heated stock - luxury indeed.

Colwick B1 No.61285 has its tender topped up with water before turning in the south locomotive servicing area at Victoria in February 1963. The snow has gone, the sun is trying to brighten the place up but the biting cold remains. Even the fireman on the tender is well wrapped up from the cold and as for splashing water - not today mate.

Two views of a local legend - no not VF - SHERWOOD FORESTER (*above*) the 'Royal Scot' numbered 46112 which spent much of its life allocated to the Western Division of the LMS before finally arriving on the Midland Lines (old Midland Division) in February 1953 albeit at Holbeck. Nevertheless, the 7P did, from thereon, make regular appearances at Nottingham (Midland) station on through expresses from St Pancras to the North. In December 1959 it finally got its transfer through to Nottingham Midland shed but by now the 4-6-0 was thirty-one years old and past its prime. When in late 1962 the LM Region authorities asked certain depots to volunteer 'Scots' for transfer to Annesley, the Midland depot at Nottingham, being neighbours and all, virtually threw the 7P over to Newstead and that is how this engine was captured alongside the massive retaining wall (I wouldn't mind a pound for every brick in... Comes to mind) at the north end of the station in February 1963. The engine is making its way to the south end to await its Marylebone working, the stock for which has yet to arrive. Note the lack of nameplates and the backing plates for said brass - who had them then? (*opposite*) A month later No.46112 was captured on film entering Victoria from the south with the morning London train. The layout of the station at this end is well depicted from a lofty vantage point - everything appears to be very neat although the 'coal carrier' is still alongside the water column on 7. Once again I ask the reader to note the deserted platforms though, admitted, it was cold.

Some months before 'Royal Scot' No.46167 THE HERTFORDSHIRE REGIMENT became a regular performer at Victoria as one of the Annesley 'Scots', it arrived one day in May 1963 to take the Up mid-morning parcels to its southbound destination. At the time it was allocated to Crewe North shed from whence it came to Annesley in September. With a full head of steam (*above*) it is seen awaiting its signal on one of the through roads on the east side of the station. The turntable is on the right of the picture, the road leading to it surrounded by ash and clinker. (*opposite*) Getting underway, the 'Scot' makes for Parliament Street bridge whilst the station pilot, a Colwick based Ivatt 'Mogul', puts a lone van into a siding.

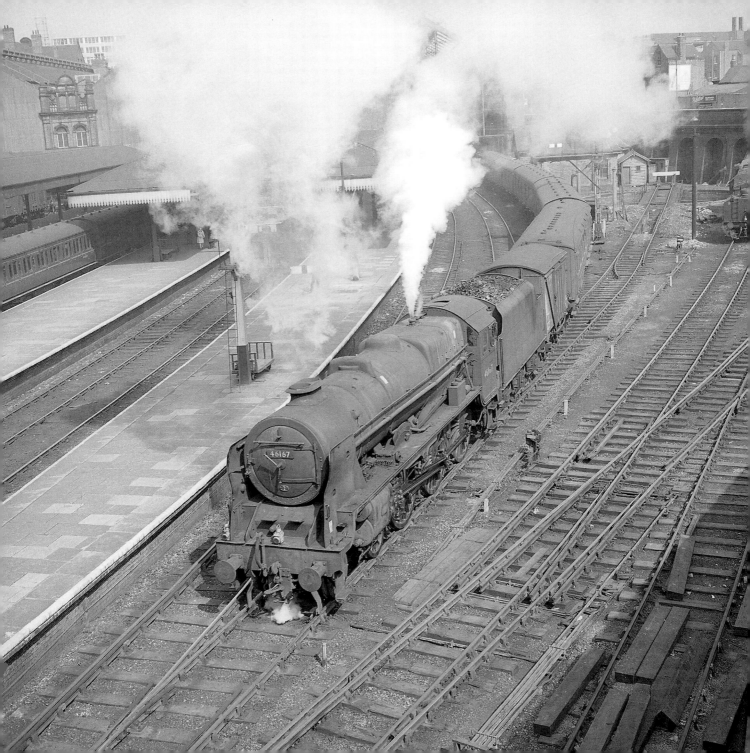

York V2 No.60895 heads the 5-15 p.m. express to Marylebone in glorious early evening sunshine in May 1963. Although stopped alongside the water column on platform 10, the 2-6-2 does not appear to have taken advantage of the facility having topped up at Annesley shed prior to making its way to Victoria for this working. The platform (*above*) is strangely quiet, even by Victoria's standards, with neither passengers, station staff, engine crew, guard or observers present in any numbers. Note the new BR Mk.1 coaches making up the bulk of the train with a similar vehicle in platform 11 - modernisation was coming to the line.

(*opposite*) A close-up of the water column which we have seen in action on numerous occasions in this section of the album. The cast iron notice reads - DRIVERS MUST NOT ALLOW WATER TO OVERFLOW ON TO PERMANENT WAY. Considering it was a year since No.60895 last had a works visit, the external condition is remarkable for the period. The engine spent all of its life working from sheds in the old North Eastern area of the LNER and later BR NE Region. York shed acquired it in July 1953 and kept it to withdrawal in October 1965. Annesley had 'borrowed' the V2 for this working - York had lots of them so they would not miss one for a few more days. Such was the state of the locomotive fleet at Annesley in those latter years that they would borrow any decent locomotive that came into their yard; if not then one of the 'Scots' would have to do but they were such rough riders.

Now here is a nice shot of a V2 which is enhanced by a Stanier 'Duchess' in the background. There were not many places where the two classes met except perhaps Perth and occasionally Aberdeen but in England it was a complete rarity. This meeting was specially arranged between the Nottingham branch of the Railway Correspondence & Travel Society and British Railways. The Pacific, No.46251 CITY OF NOTTINGHAM was the train engine for a trip undertaken by said society from Nottingham Victoria to Swindon and Eastleigh locomotive works on 9th May 1964. The V2 was apparently the stand-by engine which in the event was not required - who were these people who thought a 'semi' would need a stand-in? The event turned out to be a spectacular day for all concerned even Don Beecroft managed to get on the train and pictures of his travels to the aforementioned locomotive works will no doubt turn up in future albums planned for this series.

It is a good job that the 'Scots' had good boilers, able to generate steam quickly because this one, No.46167 has problems with leaking glands and other things, although the safety valves are happily blowing off which is a good sign. It is November 1963 - how much longer can the 'Scots' hold out ?

Weekday Cross junction, Nottingham, September 1964. This is the limit of our journey south in this album and we finish off with this unusual view of the junction here as the 5-15 p.m. Nottingham (Victoria) to Marylebone semi-fast express gets into its stride after exiting the 393 yard long Victoria Street tunnel. 'Jubilee' No.45675, with its HARDY nameplates already removed, is crossing the former Great Northern lines from Nottingham (High Level) station which is just around the curve in the tracks. Soon the London bound train will traverse the bridge over the Midland station, pass Queen's Walk goods yard and then over the viaduct spanning the Trent, after which it will accelerate all the way to Loughborough (Central), its first stop, having passed over the Midland once again, near the Brush works (at this time the Falcon facility was full of new Class 47 diesels ready to enter traffic on BR). At this time the 'Jubilee' was allocated to Leeds Holbeck shed having gone there in October 1948 from Carlisle Upperby, its only other home since new in December 1935. The 4-6-0 will continue to work until June 1967 although most of that will take place on the cross Pennine routes. Its presence on the GC main line probably stems from the fact that Annesley shed borrowed the engine from a southbound train from Yorkshire and decided to let it earn its keep for its short stay at the Nottinghamshire depot by working a London train out and back. It would be interesting to know when Holbeck had this engine back.